Be Smart About Investing

PLANNING, SAVING, AND THE STOCK MARKET

Kathiann M. Kowalski

BE SMART ABOUT MONEY AND FINANCIAL LITERACY

Enslow Publishers, Inc.
40 Industrial Road
Box 398
Berkeley Heights, NJ 07922
USA

http://www.enslow.com

This book is dedicated to my daughter, Bethany Meissner.

Copyright © 2014 by Kathiann M. Kowalski

Library of Congress Cataloging-in-Publication Data

Kowalski, Kathiann M., 1955–
  Be smart about investing : planning, saving, and the stock market / Kathiann M. Kowalski.
    pages cm. — (Be smart about money and financial literacy)
  Includes index.
  Summary: "Examines financial planning, saving, and investing, including basic methods to save money, various types of investments, strategies for investing, and the stock market"—Provided by publisher.
  Audience: Grade 9 to 12.
  ISBN 978-0-7660-4281-0
  1. Finance, Personal—Juvenile literature. 2. Investments—Juvenile literature. I. Title.
  HG179.K647 2014
  332.6—dc23
                    2013013437

Future editions:
Paperback ISBN: 978-1-4644-0505-1
EPUB ISBN: 978-1-4645-1261-2
Single-User PDF ISBN: 978-1-4646-1261-9
Multi-User PDF ISBN: 978-0-7660-5893-4

Printed in the United States of America

112013 Bang Printing, Brainerd, Minn.

10 9 8 7 6 5 4 3 2 1

Clipart Credits: Shutterstock.com.

Cover Illustration: Shutterstock.com (Alexander Hamilton) and © iStockphoto.com / Amanda Rohde (colonial suit).

Contents

Throughout the book, look for this logo 🐷 for smart financial tips and this logo 🐷 for bad choices to avoid. Also, don't forget to "Do the Math" at the end of each chapter.

Why Save?

Chapter 1

As a junior high school student, Danielle saved money from gifts so she could buy a laptop computer. A few years later, savings let her buy an iPhone.

"It's so exhilarating to know that the thing I use every day was something that I myself had bought," said the New York teen. Danielle's experiences show how saving money now can help you buy things in the future.

Eric worked summer jobs at regional theaters near his Utah home. About 90 percent of his paychecks went into a teen savings account.

"I didn't really want to have a job during school," Eric explained. "If I had spent all my money during the summer I would have been quite poor throughout my senior year of high school." Summer job savings likewise provided spending money when Eric started college.

Saving provides a financial cushion for times when money is tight. "It relieves a lot of stress to know you have enough money to get by for a little while," Eric said.

Saving also helps handle unexpected events, or contingencies. When Eric's computer suddenly needed a new video card, savings paid for it.

Investing, or using money to make money, is yet another reason to save. Some investments pay interest. Others pay out business earnings as dividends. Some types of investment also appreciate, or increase in value.

Have a Savings Plan

Danielle and Eric would not have saved any money if they spent all their earnings or monetary gifts. *Saving happens only if you spend less money than you have coming in.*

You might try to save a set percentage of income. Or, consider how much you would like to save by a certain date and then determine how much to set aside each week.

Use a budget to plan how you get and use money. You can save money, spend it, or give it away. If you're saving less than you need for your goals, revise your budget. If increasing income isn't practical, find ways to spend less.

Saving isn't always easy. In the short run, it means going without some things. In the long run, however, saving can let you buy things you might not otherwise be able to afford. Saving also provides some financial security. Together, both factors can make your life better.

Using money for one purpose means it's not available for other uses. For any financial decisions, consider the opportunity costs. How else could you be using the money? What are the pros and cons of any particular choice?

For example, spending $15 this week for a movie and snack afterward lets you have fun with friends now. However, it leaves $15 less for sports gear you want to buy next month.

Saving isn't only for adults with high-paying jobs. The longer you put off saving, the harder it will be to meet your financial goals.

Saving $10 per week will give you more than $1,000 to use two years from now. Delay a year, and you'll need twice as much each week to save the same amount. In addition, you'll miss any interest the money could have earned that first year.

Now it's your turn to "Do the Math." The end of each chapter features a math or word problem. Use what you learned in the chapter to help you answer the questions. The right math will help you make the right financial decisions.

Do the Math

Your high school is offering an educational tour of Central America next July. The tour price of $2,205 is due by June 1. When you talk with your parents on September 1, they agree to pay 60 percent of the cost if you pay the rest. Your part-time job at a supermarket provides $392 per month as take-home pay.

   a. How much must you save each month from September to May to pay your share?

   b. What percentage is that amount of your monthly take-home pay?

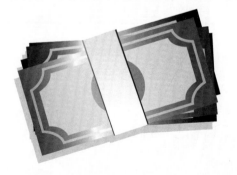

Be Smart About Investing

Saving Securely

Piggy banks are fine for spare coins, but they're not very practical. Other forms of savings offer more security, convenience, and the chance to earn interest.

Interest is a charge or fee for the temporary use of money. Usually, interest is a percentage of the principal. The principal is the amount someone borrows.

A bank deposit essentially lends funds to a bank. Interest on bank accounts pays people for letting banks use their money. Meanwhile, banks use the deposits to make more money. They invest the funds or make loans to others.

Compound interest is money earned on interest that stays in an account. Suppose a bank pays a 6 percent annual interest, compounded annually. "Compounded annually" refers to how often the bank pays interest. After one year, a savings deposit of $100 will earn $6. Leave the entire amount in the account for another year, and you'll earn 6 percent on $106. If a bank compounds interest monthly or daily, funds earn slightly more.

For example, if a bank compounds interest monthly, it pays one-twelfth the annual rate each month. If the annual rate is 6 percent, one-twelfth of that is 0.5 percent, or .005.

At a 6 percent annual interest rate, compounded monthly, $100 will earn 50¢ by the end of one month. The next month, the bank will add another 0.5 percent interest to $100.50. After twelve months, you'd have 16¢ more than you would have had without compounding.

An extra few cents may not sound like much, but it adds up. Over the years, compound interest can produce hundreds or thousands more dollars for college, a home, or retirement.

Liquidity matters, too. In other words, how easily can you convert an account or investment into cash and use it? Put another way, how long must you go without the funds? Usually, the longer you're willing to wait, the more your money can earn.

What if you tie up funds but then need the money sooner? You may have to borrow or do without something. Even if you can withdraw funds or sell an investment, you may lose interest income. You might also owe a penalty. Then you could lose part of your initial funds.

Suppose you put $5,000 into a twelve-month certificate of deposit. The certificate pays a 6 percent annual interest rate at the year's end. If you withdraw the money after three months, you might get no interest at all. If the bank also charges a fee of $25, you would have less than you started with.

Be Smart About Investing

Security is about the safety of an investment. Are you sure you will get your money back? This chapter looks at two safe groups of savings and investments: federally insured deposits and United States Treasury securities.

Money in the Bank

Four major types of bank accounts are checking accounts, savings accounts, certificates of deposit, and money market accounts. Terms for these accounts can vary greatly.

Checking accounts let you transfer money to someone else by writing a check or going online to write a check. Most checking accounts don't pay interest. Banks usually charge fees for checking account services, too.

Some banks waive basic fees for customers who do frequent business or keep large amounts on deposit. Some banks also offer free student checking accounts. These accounts are usually the best choice for teens.

Savings accounts help people save by keeping funds separate from spending money. While most savings accounts pay interest, rates have varied. In the late 1980s, many savings accounts offered 5 percent or more. As of 2012, most savings accounts paid 0.1 percent or less.

To calculate interest, multiply the principal by the interest rate. Suppose your deposit is $100, and the bank pays 5 percent interest, compounded annually. Multiply $100 by 0.05, and you get $5. If the rate was 0.1 percent, you'd multiply by 0.001. Then the same $100 would earn only 10¢ in one year.

Certificates of deposit offer a higher interest rate than regular savings accounts. However, customers must leave funds on deposit for a specific period, such as six months or a year. Afterward, many banks automatically renew the agreement unless the customer acts within several days. Withdrawals outside any such grace period usually forfeit interest or incur fees.

Money market accounts generally let people access funds quickly. They may also offer better interest rates than regular savings accounts. However, getting the best interest rate might require a large opening balance, such as $25,000 to start.

All these accounts offer a big safety benefit: insurance by the Federal Deposit Insurance Corporation (FDIC). If the bank goes out of business, the FDIC will make sure depositors get their money back, up to the limits for each account. As this book goes to press, FDIC's standard coverage was $250,000 per account holder.

Credit Unions

The National Credit Union Administration (NCUA) insures deposits of member credit unions in much the same way that the FDIC insures commercial bank deposits. While banks are for-profit corporations owned by shareholders, members generally own credit unions. Members are the credit union's customers.

Credit union members often belong to the same union, live in the same community, or share other things in common. One credit union serves federal employees in Iowa. Others are open to teamsters union members in particular states. Other credit unions serve groups of teachers.

Credit unions don't have separate shareholders demanding profits. Consequently, they might offer better interest rates or other terms than commercial banks. On the downside, credit unions may not offer as many conveniences and services. For example, credit unions may have fewer automatic teller machines (ATMs) or branches.

Saving with Uncle Sam

The United States government borrows money by issuing treasury notes, bills, or bonds. The government must eventually pay back the principal. The government pays interest, too.

Currently, the United States Treasury sells savings bonds through Treasury Direct, starting at $25. Savings bond interest is exempt from state and local taxes. Some savings bonds bought for college expenses also allow people to defer paying federal taxes until they redeem the bonds. Redeeming a savings bond before five years can forfeit some interest.

The federal government also sells treasury notes, treasury bills, and other types of bonds. The Treasury sells these securities through auctions held throughout the year. Minimum investments start at $100. Maturity terms range from a few days to thirty years.

Some treasury bills, notes, or bonds earn interest as a percentage of the face amount. The face amount is the dollar amount on the document. For example, the face amount of a $100 bond is $100. If its interest rate is 2 percent, multiply $100 by 0.02, and you get $2.

In other cases, people pay less than the face amount. Perhaps they pay $98 for a $100 bond. Their interest is the difference between the face amount and the discounted purchase price. Regardless of how Treasury securities pay interest, early redemption can forfeit interest.

People can also sell or trade some Treasury securities. For example, people buy and sell U.S. Treasury bonds on the New York Stock Exchange. If people sell bonds for more than they initially paid, they make money. If they must sell them for less, they lose money. Either way, though, the federal government will still pay whatever the bonds' terms say.

Be Smart About Investing

Compare the costs and benefits of accounts at different banking institutions. For example:

- Is the account free, or will you owe fees?
- Must you maintain a minimum balance?
- Can you withdraw money at any time?
- Will you lose interest or pay fees if you need the money before its maturity date?

Be sure to consider your savings and spending needs in the near term and for a few years into the future.

Automated teller machines (ATMs) and overdraft protection may seem to make your life easier. But "convenience" fees and penalties can be costly.

Read the fine print and terms for any bank or credit union account. Know what types of transactions incur fees. If possible, plan ahead to avoid them.

Do the Math

Big Bucks Bank imposes no service charge for a savings account if depositors also have a checking account or maintain a monthly average savings account balance of $500. Otherwise, the service charge is $5 per month. The current annual interest rate is 1 percent, compounded annually.

a. Jake deposits $600 in his Big Bucks savings account and leaves it there for three years. If interest rates don't change, how much will he have at the end of three years?

b. Sara deposits $500 in her Big Bucks savings account. At the end of one year, she withdraws $250 from savings. Sara also closes her checking account, which had a $462 balance, and spends the cash. If Sara makes no other deposits or withdrawals for another year, how much will she pay in service charges?

c. Andrea withdraws $40 from her Big Bucks checking account at the XYZ Bank's ATM. She forgets that Big Bucks Bank charges a $5 fee for ATM transactions at other banks. What percent of her $40 withdrawal is Andrea's ATM fee?

Be Smart About Investing

Risky Business

Do you want to own a bit of Microsoft or McDonald's? Would you like to invest in a growing company?

The New York Stock Exchange, NASDAQ, and other exchanges are marketplaces for buying and selling securities. Securities are stocks, bonds, and other easily traded investments.

Sometimes securities investments earn interest. In other cases, investors get payouts from company earnings called dividends. People also gain or lose money by selling securities. Most investors aim to buy at a low price. They prefer to sell when the price is high.

Securities investments can yield good returns. However, you must be careful. Investing in securities is risky business.

Stocks, Bonds, and Commodities

Generally, the more potential there is for making money, the more risk there is if things go wrong. An investment's form can also affect its risk level.

Bonds are basically IOUs. A bond's terms define its interest rate and repayment terms. A city might issue bonds for $500 each and promise to repay the amount plus 3 percent interest in five years. Or, a company might issue $1,000 bonds and promise to repay the amount plus 4 percent annual interest in two years.

In these examples, the city and the company are the bonds' issuers. If a private company goes bankrupt or out of business, bondholders usually get paid before stockholders, but after some other creditors.

Stockholders or shareholders are the owners of a for-profit corporation. Many stockholders are individuals. They may be people like yourself or your parents. Some stockholders may work at the company. Corporations can also own stock in other companies. Two basic kinds of stock are preferred stock and common stock.

Preferred stock owners often get a set dividend based on the stock's face value. For example, $100 of preferred stock might pay a set amount of $5 per year. If the company goes out of business, owners of preferred stock get money back before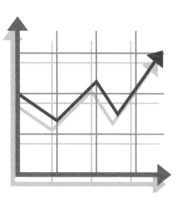

other stockholders. However, preferred stockholders usually have no say in the company's actions. For example, they don't vote on company leadership.

Common stock offers more financial upside and downside than preferred stock. If a company earns a lot of money, the dividend payout can be bigger. The stock price on the market also tends to rise when company earnings improve.

Stockholders with common stock also have a say in how the company is run. They can vote for company directors—the people who make major decisions. They also vote on some corporate actions. One example might be whether to merge, or join with, another business.

Commodities investors rarely use the bulk items they buy. Rather, they're buying on speculation. For a nonperishable commodity, like gold, the investor bets that the price will go up over time.

For agricultural goods, investors usually buy commodities futures. They agree to buy or sell an amount of the commodity at a set price on a specific future date. Essentially, they're betting on whether the price will go up or down.

Depending on how the market price changes, investors can gain or lose lots of money. Suppose someone agrees to buy five thousand bushels of corn six months from now for $2 per bushel. The investor won't use the corn. Instead, he or she will resell it at the going price. If the market price rises to $3 per bushel six months from now, the investor can resell the corn and make a profit of $5,000. If the price drops to $1.50 per bushel, however, the buyer under the contract would still have to pay $2. The buyer would then lose $2,500 when he or she resold the corn.

Day traders may own securities for a few seconds or a few hours. They gamble that small swings in market price will produce profits. However, day traders can also suffer huge losses and incur debts. Day trading is even riskier if people buy stocks with borrowed money.

Risky, Riskier, and Riskiest

What can go wrong with securities investments? Plenty!

Many factors can change a company's value. New competitors may enter the market. If another company's laptop computers got a majority of the market share, for example, Capable Computer's profits could dip. Then its stock price might drop.

Other things can also go wrong. Managers can make bad decisions. Relationships with key customers or suppliers could sour. Raw material prices may go up. Legal claims, credit problems, and other issues may arise.

Even if a company's overall value doesn't change, stock prices fluctuate. They rise and fall in unpredictable ways. If more people want to buy a stock than are currently selling it, the market price rises. Conversely, if more people want to sell a stock than are looking to buy it, the price drops.

Spread the Risk

An old adage says not to put all your eggs in one basket. The idea applies to investing, too. When investors diversify, they have a variety of investments. They might buy stocks or bonds in many different companies, for example. Alternatively, they might own stocks in different companies, as well as bonds from municipalities, or other types of investments.

If any one security loses value, the investor loses something. However, the chance that all securities will lose value at the same time is small. Diversification spreads the risk of losses so there is less chance of losing everything.

For this reason, *Wall Street Journal* financial writer Karen Blumenthal recommends that beginning investors start with mutual funds. A mutual fund pools money from many people. It uses that money to buy and sell securities from multiple sources. In this way, mutual funds spread risk among many investments. They minimize risks if any single investment goes bad.

Nonetheless, any mutual fund is only as good as the investments it holds. Some mutual funds focus on municipal bonds or shares in large, established corporations. They involve less risk than ones that invest in small, start-up companies or junk bonds. Junk bonds have high interest rates but also very high risk.

Fund management matters, too. When you decide to invest in any mutual fund, you agree to let the fund managers make day-to-day investment decisions. Read about any fund's management before trusting them with your money. Indeed, do your homework before making any investment decision!

Before putting money into the stock market, consider when you need it out. You'd rather not have to sell and take a loss when normal market fluctuations cause a slight downturn. Financial writer Karen Blumenthal at the *Wall Street Journal* recommends putting any money that you'll need within three years into safer, more stable money market or savings accounts.

Don't forget taxes when making investment decisions. While some bonds are exempt from certain taxes, most investment income is taxable at the federal and state levels. Different rates can apply, depending on the type of investment income and how long you own the investment.

GOOD ¢

NON ¢

Do the Math

Diluted earnings per share (diluted EPS) equals a company's annual earnings divided by the sum of all outstanding common stock shares and other shares the company might issue because of stock options. Suppose a company has 90,000 shares of outstanding common stock, but contracts with employees might cause it to issue another 10,000 shares. If the company earned $1 million last year, its diluted EPS is $1 million divided by 100,000, or $10.

Review diluted EPS and other financial data to gauge a company's performance. The graph at right shows hypothetical data for four fictitious companies. Numbers in brackets show each company's current stock price.

a. Which company had the greatest percentage growth in diluted EPS from 2013 to 2015?

b. Which company's 2015 diluted EPS represents the largest percentage of its current stock price? Why might investors care about that?

Be Smart About Investing

Diluted Earnings Per Share

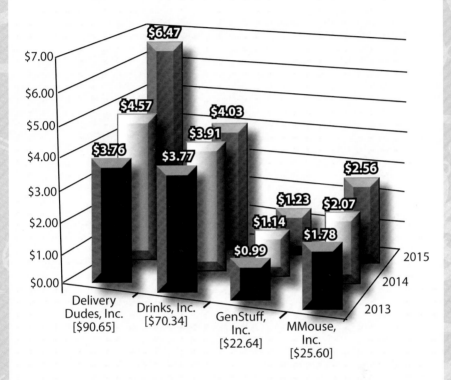

Do Your Homework!

Before buying a new smartphone or laptop computer, you would probably read reviews and compare features. Use the same care when investing your money.

Understand the Marketplace

You will need to buy most securities through an exchange or broker. A broker is someone who buys and sells securities on behalf of others, subject to various laws and regulations. Choices range from bare-bones online brokers to firms with individual investment advisers. In general, the more service you get, the more you'll pay.

Pay attention to all fees and other costs. Transaction fees are flat fees or commissions charged for completing a purchase or sale of securities.

Be Smart About Investing

A mutual fund's load is the company's fee for managing the fund. No load mutual funds don't charge separate management fees. Their asset price usually covers payment for the fund manager's services.

Required Reading

Thanks to the Internet, many documents are available online from different companies or government agencies. Review that information and use it when investing.

By law, most entities must provide a prospectus when they offer securities for sale. Among other things, the prospectus tells who is issuing, or offering, the securities. Is the issuer an established company or a new business? Or, is it a city or other government body?

The prospectus describes the issuer's activities. It also talks about risks when the securities were first sold. Pay extra attention here!

Think of an annual report as a company's yearly financial report card. Quarterly reports provide more up-to-date information. What trends does the company's performance show? What factors affect its income?

Proxy statements describe matters up for shareholder voting. Giving your proxy to a company's representatives lets them cast your vote at an upcoming shareholder meeting. For example, a proxy statement might seek support for certain director candidates. Or, it might ask for your vote on a proposed merger or spin-off. Proxy statements give potential investors insight about what's going on at the company.

Dig deeper. Do you read movie critics' reviews before deciding to see a new film? Companies like Moody's and Standard & Poor's provide a similar service for investors. They rate securities based on the issuer's financial health.

Keep Current

You may or may not ever have a huge investment portfolio. However, you should always keep current on financial and other news. Read the business sections of newspapers and magazines. Which events might affect the value of your investments?

Has a company made a new discovery or increased its market share? Did a big deal go through or fall apart? Has a lawsuit been filed or resolved? Has upper management changed?

More generally, watch for upward or downward trends in different industries. The more you know about what's going on in the business world, the better you can watch out for your financial future.

Track your investments' value over time with computer spreadsheets. Just remember that unless a company pays interest or a dividend, you won't realize, or actually incur, a gain or loss until you sell securities. Thus, you're not automatically rich if your investments' value goes up on paper. Nor are you suddenly poor if your stocks' prices dip temporarily.

No investment is worth it if makes you lose sleep at night. Avoid any investment that makes you uneasy, even if someone says it's a great deal.

Stockbroker Bernie Madoff bilked investors out of more than $21 billion. To attract and keep clients, he reported high investment yields that didn't exist. When some investors wanted to withdraw the fake gains, Madoff paid them by stealing from other accounts. The more Madoff tried to cover up his lies, the more he kept stealing.

Madoff's swindle was a Ponzi scheme. Con artist Charles Ponzi made this type of scam infamous in the 1920s. Someone offers consistently high investment returns. The swindler pays phony "profits" to a few people with other people's money. Those people talk about their good fortune, and more people invest with the crook. In the end, most people lose money.

Do Your Homework!

In 2009, Madoff pled guilty to eleven felonies. A federal court sentenced him to 150 years. Later, Madoff called his victims "greedy." Sophisticated banks and hedge funds should have done more due diligence, he told *New York Magazine* reporter Steve Fishman. Even individual investors should have suspected problems, Madoff argued. "Their friends had told them, 'How can you be making 15 or 18 percent when everyone is making less money?'"

Nothing excuses Madoff. Nonetheless, greed should never get in the way of good judgment. If something sounds too good to be true, it is!

Be Smart About Investing

Do the Math

Zynga Inc. designs and runs online social games, such as Farmville. In December 2011, Zynga's initial public offering (IPO) sold 100 million shares of common stock for $10 each. Shares then traded on the NASDAQ stock exchange under the symbol ZNGA.

a. Review Zynga's July 1, 2011, Form S-1 Registration Statement and Prospectus, especially the discussion of risk factors. Would you have bought Zynga stock in the IPO? Find the prospectus by searching online for "SEC zynga registration statement 2011.gov" or go to <http://www.sec.gov> and use their search tools to find the Zynga prospectus.

b. On October 23, 2012, Zynga announced it would lay off some workers, close two foreign studios, and shut down thirteen older games. The next day, Zynga shares fell to $2.10. What percentage was that of the initial $10 price? If you bought 200 shares of Zynga stock in the IPO and sold them at the $2.10 price, how much would you have lost from your initial investment?

c. Suppose you bought 300 shares of Zynga at $2.10 on October 24, 2012, and sold them for $2.39 on October 25, 2012. What would your gain have been before any transaction or broker fees?

d. Find out if Zynga stock is still publicly traded. Check your newspaper's business section, or run an online search for "Zynga stock price," and see if the price is current. If Zynga is still traded, what is the current price per share? If you bought 100 shares at $4 per share and sold them today, how much would you gain or lose?

Do Your Homework!

The Government's

Role

Chapter
5

The United States economy is mostly a free market system. For the most part, it relies on supply and demand. However, the system needs rules. Otherwise, many people would cheat others, and the whole system could suffer.

Modern financial regulation began in the early twentieth century. Congress set up the Federal Reserve Bank in 1913, and the "Fed" is still the United States' central bank. As a quasi-governmental agency, the Fed sets monetary policy. It issues paper money, regulates national banks, lends to banks in emergencies, and does other jobs.

Unfortunately, banks and financial markets still had problems. They needed more rules.

Depression–Era Legislation

Many banks failed during the Great Depression (1929–1933). As a result, people lost their life's savings.

Be Smart About Investing

The Banking Act of 1933 set up the Federal Deposit Insurance Corporation (FDIC) to insure bank deposits. That same year, the Glass-Steagall Act limited banks' dealings in securities.

Congress also regulated the stock market. The Securities Act of 1933 forbids fraud in selling securities. The law also makes issuers give information to potential investors.

The Securities Exchange Act of 1934 set up the Securities and Exchange Commission (SEC). Organizations must file prospectuses and various reports with the agency.

Additional laws in 1939 and 1940 extended rules to bond issuers and mutual funds. Various regulations also apply to investment advisers. A 2002 law expanded corporate disclosure requirements and rules on accounting.

Together, these laws make sure investors can get information. The laws also forbid various types of cheating. One example is insider trading—dealing in securities with confidential information that the public doesn't know.

The Financial Crisis and New Laws

As the twentieth century ended, banks and other companies extended more and more credit. At the same time, banks became more active in buying and selling securities. Banks began "bundling" mortgage and other debt obligations. Meanwhile, banks expanded nationwide and internationally.

Then a housing price bubble burst early in the twenty-first century. Refinancing of mortgages became harder. More and more people defaulted on mortgages. Securities based on those debts lost value.

In 2008, the financial house of cards collapsed. Companies like Citicorp and the AIG insurance company needed government help to survive. Lehman Brothers, a large investment firm, filed for bankruptcy.

The failure of large financial firms scared banks. They became reluctant to lend to each other. Banks also made fewer loans to customers.

Many businesses suffered cash flow problems when they couldn't get short-term loans. Layoffs and business failures followed.

In 2010, Congress passed the Dodd-Frank Wall Street Reform and Consumer Protection Act. The law aims to fix problems that let many debtors get in over their heads. Among other things, the law expanded federal regulation of banks and securities markets. It also created the federal Financial Stability Oversight Council and an independent Bureau of Consumer Financial Protection within the Federal Reserve. The law's success will depend on rules and the government's enforcement policies.

Government laws and regulations can help you. Know what information you should review when investing money. You can also seek agency help if problems arise. The SEC investigates and sues companies that violate its laws. The Bureau of Consumer Financial Protection can help with questions about banking services or fees.

Be Smart About Investing

Legally required disclosures only help if people read and consider them when making financial decisions. Review documents and consider risks carefully.

Don't assume that the government guards all your interests. Laws impose some rules on companies that buy and sell securities. Unfortunately, the law cannot stop people from making poor choices about their money. Even when companies obey the law, you must watch out for your savings and investments.

Do the Math

Among other things, federal securities laws forbid using inside information to deal in publicly traded securities. Inside information is nonpublic information known by or gained from someone with a duty to keep it confidential. Violations of the law can result in imprisonment and criminal penalties.

Suppose MegaCompany president Bud Badactor learns that defects in its products cause serious illness. Mega-Company will face many lawsuits.

The board of directors decides to recall the affected products. Just before the announcement, Badactor sells five thousand shares of company stock at $15 per share. Within hours of the recall, MegaCompany stock falls to $3 per share. How much illegal gain has Bud Badactor realized from insider trading?

Be Smart About Investing

Taking Stock

General economic and financial developments can influence the stock market—and vice versa. The Great Depression of the 1930s began when stock prices plummeted on Black Thursday, October 24, 1929. By the time the market hit bottom in 1933, most stocks had barely a fifth of their earlier value.

Stock market crashes don't happen only in distant history. The Dow Jones Industrial Average combines information for about thirty large companies. On October 18, 1987, the Dow dropped almost 23 percent. On September 29, 2008, the Dow's value dropped about $1.2 trillion in a single day.

Political and legal events sometimes influence the stock market. In 2011, President Barack Obama proposed a $447 billion economic stimulus plan. The Dow plunged 304 points the next day.

Even the weather can affect stock market prices! One study by researchers at The Ohio State University and the University of Michigan found that stock markets often gave investors better returns on sunny days.

In any case, no one can say exactly how the stock market will perform on any day. The world is never totally predictable. Thus, the stock market always involves risk.

Doing "Nothing" Has Risks

Reading about risky investments sounds scary. Bank and credit union fees can seem costly. However, hiding your loot at home isn't the answer.

If you don't invest any money, it can't earn any interest or dividends. Nor can you profit from selling it later. Meanwhile, inflation can erode your money's value.

Inflation is a general decrease in the dollar's purchasing power. Suppose the annual inflation rate is 2 percent. All else being equal, something that cost $100 this year would cost $102 a year later.

Historically, inflation has run much higher. The overall inflation rate during the 1970s was 6.8%. But several periods in that decade saw double-digit inflation. From 1979 to 1980, the annual inflation rate was 13.5 percent. Suppose you were buying school supplies. You would need $113.50 in 1980 dollars to buy the same items that $100 could have bought in 1979.

Inflation makes prices rise. However, people's income doesn't automatically rise as fast or as much. Thus, inflation can weaken your purchasing power.

Investing wisely can provide a hedge against inflation. Deciding on the best approach, however, requires careful consideration and sound judgment.

Look at the Long Term

At age twelve, Laura used gift money to purchase some PepsiCo stock. Many of Laura's friends liked the company's products. In addition, she figured people would always want sodas and snacks. More than fifteen years later, Laura sold some of the stock when she and her new husband bought a home.

"When I decided with my parents to buy PepsiCo stock, I definitely wasn't thinking about buying a house or getting married," Laura wrote in *Odyssey* magazine. Yet her investment had nearly tripled over the years. And Laura could use the funds when she needed them.

You're probably not thinking seriously about marriage, home ownership, or kids yet. Retirement probably seems eons away! The sooner you start saving and investing, though, the better you'll be able to handle these financial challenges when they arise.

Indeed, if you wait until you're rich to start saving, you probably won't save or get rich. Begin saving regularly now as part of your budget plan. Over time, even small amounts will add up. And you'll make a sound investment in your future.

GOOD 👍

When it comes to saving and investments, invest your time as well as your money. Consider investment decisions carefully and review them periodically.

Never buy into any investment unless you understand what it is and how it is supposed to work. A derivative security is an investment whose value depends on one or more underlying assets, such as stocks or bonds. Many derivative securities sold before the 2008 financial crisis were shares in bundles of bad mortgage debts. As debtors defaulted, the securities lost value.

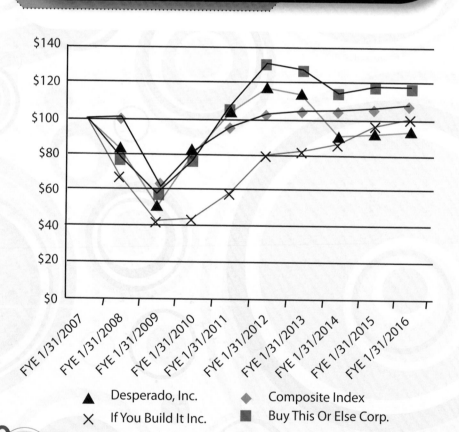

Legend:
- ▲ Desperado, Inc.
- ✕ If You Build It Inc.
- ◆ Composite Index
- ■ Buy This Or Else Corp.

Be Smart About Investing

Do the Math

In the real world, composite indices like the S&P 500 Index and the Dow Jones Industrial Index combine information for dozens or even hundreds of companies. Suppose the graph on page 40 represents several companies' performances relative to a composite index of two hundred key industrial corporations. All companies and this index are fictional.

The graph assumes that $100 was invested in each company's common stock on the last trading day in January of each year. (FYE means "fiscal year ending.") The graph also assumes that any dividends were reinvested in the company.

a. What might explain the drop for all three companies and the Composite Index as of early 2009?

b. Suppose Bob bought $5,500 worth of If You Build It Inc. common stock on January 31, 2007. About how much would he have lost if he sold all the shares on January 31, 2012?

c. Which stocks performed worse than the Composite Index from January 2014 to January 2016? Which did better?

Glossary

appreciation— An increase in value over time.

checking account—Bank arrangement that allows customers to transfer account funds by writing checks or going online.

commission—Percentage-based fee.

commodities—Marketable items.

contingency—An unexpected event.

credit union—Financial institution operated for its members' benefit.

day traders—People who buy and sell many securities throughout the day, hoping to profit from price swings.

depreciation—Loss in value over time.

diversify—To invest money in multiple ways, thereby spreading the risk of loss.

dividend—Distribution of business earnings.

due diligence—Detailed investigation of business records and activities before a transaction.

inflation—Decrease in a currency's purchasing power over time.

insider trading—Dealing in securities with nonpublic information known by or gained from someone with a duty to keep it confidential.

Be Smart About Investing

interest—Payment or charge for the use of money.

investment—Use of money or property in hopes of financial gain.

junk bonds—High-risk debt instruments.

liquidity—Ease of converting assets into cash.

load—Fee for managing a mutual fund.

money market account—Bank account whose funds are in liquid, secure investments, such as treasury bonds, bills, and notes.

mutual fund—Investment that pools money from many investors to trade in a variety of securities.

opportunity costs—Uses for money that one gives up by using funds for another purpose.

principal—Amount of a loan or investment.

prospectus—Information booklet describing business activities and risks of a securities purchase.

transaction fees—Charges for buying or selling securities.

proxy statement—Material asking shareholders to let others cast their vote a certain way on corporate matters.

realize—To incur a gain or loss in the real world.

securities—Stocks, bonds, commodities, and other easily traded investments.

Learn More

Books

Blumenthal, Karen. *The Wall Street Journal Guide to Starting Your Financial Life*. New York: Three Rivers Press, 2009.

Connolly, Sean. *The Stock Market*. Mankato, Minn.: Amicus, 2011.

Heath, Julia. *Saving and Investing*. New York: Facts on File, Inc., 2012.

Lawless, Robert. *The Student's Guide to Financial Literacy*. Westport, Conn.: Greenwood, 2010.

North, Charles, and Charles Caes. *The Stock Market*. New York: Rosen Publishing Group, 2012.

Be Smart About Investing

Internet Addresses

CNN Money: Money 101—Financial Advice and Lessons Made Easy
<http://money.cnn.com/magazines/moneymag/money101/>

Investor.gov (Securities and Exchange Commission): For Students
<http://investor.gov/classroom/students#other%20topics>

Junior Achievement Student Center
<http://studentcenter.ja.org/Pages/default.aspx>

Do the Math Answer Key

Chapter 1: Why Save?

a. If your parents pay 60 percent, your 40 percent share of $2,205 comes to $882 (2,205 x .04). Divide by 9 months, and you need $98 per month.

b. $98 is 25 percent of $392.

Chapter 2: Saving Securely

a. $618.18.

At the end of the first year, he'll have $606: $600 + (.01 × $600). At the end of the second year, he'll have $612.06: $606 + (.01 × $606).By the end of the third year, he'll have $618.18: $612.06 + (.01 × $612.06)

b. $60.00. Sara earned 1 percent on the $500 for the first year, so she had a balance of $505 before withdrawing $250. That left $255 in the savings account. With no other deposits, she did not have $500 in either checking or savings. At $5 per month Sara would pay $60 in fees to keep the savings account open.

c. $5 is 12.5 percent of $40.

Chapter 3: Risky Business

a. Delivery Dudes, Inc. had the largest percentage growth in diluted EPS. The difference between the 2015 diluted EPS of $6.47 and the 2013 diluted EPS of $3.76 is $2.71. That is about 72 percent of the 2013 diluted EPS.

b. MMouse, Inc.: In 2015, the $2.56 diluted EPS for MMouse, Inc. was 10 percent of its $25.60 stock price. Figures like this help gauge potential returns on investment—either through dividends or through a higher price when someone sells the stock. If other factors are equal, the higher percentage suggests that the stock is a good value for its price.

Chapter 4: Do Your Homework!

a. Answers will vary. In any case, notice how many risk factors are noted—and how many are not within Zynga's sole control.

b. $2.10 is 21 percent of the initial $10 price. If you'd bought 200 shares for $10 each and sold them for $2.10, you'd lose $1,580, or 79 percent of your initial investment. Any broker fees or transaction costs would be extra.

c. If you bought 300 shares of stock at $2.10, your total investment would be $630. If you sold those shares the next day for $2.39 per share, you'd gain 300 times 29¢, which is $87. Any broker fees or transaction costs would reduce your profit.

d. If Zynga is still publicly traded, find the current stock price in the *Wall Street Journal* or Google "NASDAQ ZYNGA." Multiply that price by 100 to find the current price for 100 shares. Then subtract $400, which is the price for 100 shares at $4 per share. A positive number represents a gain. A negative number would be a loss.

Chapter 5: The Government's Role

By acting on the information before it became public, Bud Badactor got $15 per share, instead of $3 per share. That's a difference of $12 per share. Multiply $12 by 5,000, and Badactor's insider trading got him $60,000 more than he would have had if he hadn't acted on the inside information.

Chapter 6: Taking Stock

a. As discussed in Chapter 5, a financial crisis hit in 2008. Many stocks lost value in the months that followed.

b. Bob would have lost 20 percent of his investment because, as of January 31, 2012, the value of If You Build It Inc. stock was only 80 percent of its value as of January 31, 2007. Multiply $5,500 by 0.20, and you get a loss of $1,100.

c. In this hypothetical, Desperado, Inc. and If You Build It Inc. did worse than the composite index for the period from January 2014 to January 2016. Buy This Or Else Corp. performed better.

Do the Math Answer Key

Index

Be Smart About Investing